Little Saint Therese
Grows Up

Little Saint Therese Grows Up

by
Margaret Mary Myers

Cover Picture by
Michele Cullen Crocco

ISBN: 9798464388796
Printed in the United States of America

You can see my book listings at:
Amazon.com/author/margaretmarymyers

Table of Contents

1 Little Therese Liked to Play   6

2 Therese and her Family Went on Picnics   8

3 Little Therese Recited Poems   10

4 Therese Went Fishing with her Papa   12

5 Therese Visits Jesus in the Church   14

6 Therese had a Puppy Named Tom   16

7 Little Therese Enjoyed her Birds   18

8 Therese Liked to go to Church   20

9 Therese and her Family Prayed the Rosary   22

10 Therese Liked to go to the Beach   24

11 Therese Liked to Think about Heaven   26

12 Therese Liked to Learn   28

13 Therese Made her First Holy Communion   30

14 Therese went to See the Pope   32

15 Therese became a Nun   34

16 Therese Set up the Altar for Jesus   36

17 Therese Taught the Sisters her Little Way   38

1) Little Therese Liked to Play

You probably like to play with toys and games. Did you know that the saints liked toys and games too? The Little Saint Therese may have played with some of the same things that you do.

Out of doors she liked to swing and to skip rope. Little Therese also had dolls, a spinning top, a tiny wheelbarrow, and other toys.

Do you know what Therese enjoyed most of all? She enjoyed setting up her little altar. She had little candlesticks, little statues and a little missal. She even had a tiny chalice, such as the priest uses in the Mass. "Papa!" she would call, after she had set up her little altar. And how pleased she was as her father admired her work of art.

2) Therese and Her Family Went on Picnics

Have you ever been on a picnic? Little Therese and her family often went on summer picnics in the country.

Her older sisters would sit with her mother under the trees. They would sew or knit. They would talk about happy things. Her father would fish.

Little Therese and her sisters would joyfully gather flowers. They liked the fields of cornflowers and brightly colored poppies. They liked the wide open spaces and the big trees.

All these beautiful things made Therese think of the good God who made them all.

3) Little Therese Recited Poems

The mother of Little Therese wrote many letters. When Therese was four years old, her mother wrote this:

"She will be good. You can see the good there already. She talks of nothing but God. She would not miss her little prayers for anything in the world.

"I wish you could hear Therese reciting little fables. I have never seen anything so pretty. She finds out the expression and tone she should use, all by herself! But it is especially when she says:

'Say, little one with golden head, Where dwelleth God, think you? O, everywhere in all the world, Then in the heaven so blue.' "

4) Saint Therese Went Fishing with Her Papa

Have you ever been fishing? When Saint Therese was a little girl sometimes she would go fishing with her Papa. Little Therese and her Papa would take a picnic basket with bread and jam. Sometimes Therese would try fishing with a small fishing rod of her own. Often she would sit on the grass and think lovingly of Heaven and the good God.

One day clouds darkened the lovely blue sky and there was a big thunderstorm. Saint Therese said later that a thunderbolt fell in a field close by. She said, "Far from being the least bit frightened, I was overjoyed – God seemed so near."

Papa picked up Therese to carry her home, along with his fishing tackle.

5) Therese Visits Jesus in the Church

"Each afternoon I went with Papa for a walk," wrote Little Therese.

Therese and her Papa would go to churches where they could visit the dear Little Jesus hidden in the tabernacle. Some days they would go to one church and some days to another one. Sometimes they would visit the chapel of the Carmelite Convent.

"Look, little Queen!" said Papa. "There are holy nuns who are always praying to Almighty God."

Years later, Little Therese would become one of those nuns.

6) Therese Had a Puppy Named Tom

One day Papa brought Little Therese a big surprise! Hidden in a box was her own little puppy, whining to come out and play. Out jumped Tom, a little white cocker spaniel. Therese thanked her father with a delighted hug.

After that Tom went with them on their afternoon walks. He would lie outside the church and wait while they prayed. He would happily wag his little tail when they came out.

Little Therese loved her little dog, Tom, very much.

7) Little Therese Enjoyed Her Birds

Therese had different kinds of birds. She had doves. Have you ever heard the pretty cooing sounds that doves make?

She had parrots. They are big, colorful birds that can repeat what you say.

Therese had canaries. Canaries sing pretty little songs.

One time Little Therese adopted a tiny baby bird called a linnet. It didn't have its parents to learn from, so it tried to imitate the songs of a canary. Therese said it was hard for a linnet with a sweet little voice to sing the beautiful, strong sounds of a canary. But it tried and tried. Finally it could sing just like a canary. Therese was happy and surprised to hear it singing.

8) Therese Liked to Go to Church

The first sermon that Therese understood was about the sufferings of Jesus. After that, she listened to all the sermons.

During the sermon, little Therese would sometimes look at the kind, holy face of her dear Papa.

When Therese made her first Confession, her big sister Pauline helped her get ready. Years later, Saint Therese told her sister, "You told me that it was not to a man but to God himself that I was going to tell my sins. I came out of the confessional feeling more light hearted and happy than ever before."

9) Therese and Her FamilyPrayed the Rosary

Each evening the family gathered near the statue of Blessed Mother in the living room to pray the Rosary.

Therese later wrote: "My place was beside our beloved Father. I had but to look at Papa to learn how the saints pray."

Also, in the evening, there would be a game of checkers. After that, big sisters Marie or Pauline would read to the family.

Therese later wrote, "During this time, I always sat on Papa's knee. When the reading was over, he would rock me gently, my head pillowed on his breast. He would sing in his beautiful voice, some soothing melody as if to lull me to sleep."

10) Therese Went to the Beach

When Therese was about six years old, she saw the ocean for the first time. She wrote later, "Its majesty and the roaring of the waves spoke to my soul of God's power and greatness."

Another time, when Therese was seven, her Papa had gone to the beach. She wrote in her exercise book: "Perhaps he will bring me back some crabs. I shall be so glad, for it is so amusing to see the little black creatures become red when they are cooked!"

When Therese was 12, her aunt took her and her sisters once again to the seaside. They enjoyed the beach with their cousins. They enjoyed catching shrimp. And they had fun riding donkeys.

11) Therese Liked to Think About Heaven

Sometimes Little Therese would go to her cousins' house. Then her Papa would come to walk her home. Therese looked up at the dark sky. She saw in the stars what looked like a letter "T". "Look, Papa!" she said, "my name is written in heaven."

One day Pauline wanted to teach Little Therese something about heaven. Pauline sent Therese to get Papa's big drinking glass. Next to it, Pauline put Therese's tiny thimble. She then filled them both with water. She asked Therese which seemed fuller, the drinking glass or the thimble. Little Therese said that one was as full as the other. It was not possible to pour more water into either of them.

Pauline had shown her that everyone in heaven is FILLED with happiness.

12) Therese Liked to Learn

Therese liked to read very much. For several years she was taught at home. She liked to learn and she studied hard.

At the end of each school year would be prize day. Little Therese would be dressed all in white. The house would be decorated with flowers and branches. Her relatives and friends would come for the event. Her father would give her the prizes.

Therese later wrote about this day, "My heart beat fast as I listened to my notes and received the prizes in the presence of the whole family, from the hands of my 'King'. To me it was a picture of Judgment Day!"

13) Therese Made Her First Holy Communion

Little Therese got ready carefully for her First Holy Communion.

Let us read what Therese wrote about her First Holy Communion: "At last there dawned the most beautiful day of all the days of my life.

"I remember our entrance into the chapel and the melody of the morning hymn, 'O Altar of God, where the Angels are hovering.'

"How sweet was the first embrace of Jesus! It was indeed an act of love." I said, 'I love Thee, and I give myself to Thee forever.' Tears of happiness welled up and overflowed. Joy alone, a joy too deep for words, overflowed within me."

14) Therese Went to See the Pope

Therese loved Jesus more and more. She wanted to become a nun and spend lots of time in church with Jesus, and she wanted to pray for people.

When Therese was a teenager, she wanted to become a nun soon. She did not want to wait for many years. Her father took her to ask the bishop. She put her hair up and tried to look very grown up. The kind bishop smiled. He told her he would see.

Then Papa took Therese on a train trip to see the Pope. She asked the Pope if she could be a nun. The Holy Father blessed Therese. He said, "You will enter if it be God's will."

15) Therese Became a Nun

Therese was soon allowed to enter the Carmelite convent. Jesus had said yes to her prayer to become a nun while still a teenage girl.

"I have come to save souls and especially to pray for priests," thought Saint Therese. Of course, we can pray for priests, and for our families and other people, too.

Therese walked into the church in a beautiful white velvet dress with rich lace. Her long golden hair hung over her shoulders as she walked down the aisle with her beloved father. Then she put on the Carmelite dress.

As Therese walked back to the convent, she saw snow on the ground. She felt it was a gift from the Holy Child Jesus for her special day. How happy she was!

16) Therese Set up the Altar for Jesus

Sister Therese had many different duties in the convent at different times. At one time she had the job of answering the door.

One day, when Sister Therese opened the door to let some workmen in, do you know who followed them? Tom, her faithful old dog! I wonder if she was surprised to see him!

Do you remember the favorite toy of Little Therese? It was her little altar set. Now she was asked to set up the real altar for Jesus to come in Mass each day. She said, "I rejoiced in being able to prepare the altar linen on which Our Lord was to be laid."

17) Therese Taught the Sisters Her Little Way

Sister Therese sometimes helped care for the sick Sisters. When an older nun was impatient with her, Therese was kind to the older nun for love of Jesus.

Therese also taught the new Sisters in the convent how to be good Sisters. She taught them her "little way".

We sometimes hear about saints who did great things. But Sister Therese taught the new Sisters that they didn't have to do great things to become a saint. They just needed to love Jesus in the little things of day to day life. She wanted them to trust in Jesus. She wanted them to know how very much Jesus loves them.

Even though Saint Therese grew up, we still call her "Little Saint Therese" because of her "little way" of love.

Prayer for a Child to Little Saint Therese:

Dear Saint Therese, please help me to know how much Jesus loves me. Help me to love Him every day. Amen.

A FEW WORDS TO THE PARENTS

Hopefully, older children will enjoy the book, but the reading level was specifically designed for children of a second or third grade reading level to read to a parent, grandparent, or another loving person in his or her life who can help with the harder words.

If you don't know the life of St. Therese well, you might not have known that her mother died when she was very young. I chose not to include that in this story for young children, but that is why her mother was not included in the story except when St. Therese was very young.

St. Therese is written "Thérèse" in the original French, and some people write and say it this way. I chose the American version.

Nothing has been fictionized in this book. In quotations, a few words or phrases have occasionally been omitted to make the reading simpler or the meaning clearer for young children, but without altering the meaning or context.

It is my hope that this book will help your child learn to love Saint Therese more, and thus, also, to love Our Lord more.

Information was obtained from the following biographical books:
1) Autobiography of St. Therese, translated by the Reverend Thomas N. Taylor, 1927.
2) Collected Little Flower Works, by the Reverend Albert H. Dolan, O.Carm., 1929.
3) Louis Martin, An Ideal Father, by Louis and Marjorie Wust, 1953.
4) The Story of a Family, by Stephane-Joseph Piat, O.F.M., 1948.

Printed in Great Britain
by Amazon